# The Baptism in the

# Holy Spirit

# &

# The Benefits of Speaking in Tongues

## CHERRI CAMPBELL

Victorious Faith Publishing
info@victoriousfaith.co

ISBN: 978-1-951800-03-1  (Paperback)

# Contents

# Contents

# Chapter One

# The Baptism in the Holy Spirit

A s God has called me to a traveling teaching ministry, I have had the blessing and privilege of teaching in many, many churches, even in many different Christian denominations. One of the things God has called me to teach on is the baptism in the Holy Spirit with speaking in tongues. I have found that the biggest reason many Christians have not received the baptism in the Holy Spirit is simply because they don't understand it and have wrong ideas about it. There is a great lack of knowledge among many Christians about this very important gift from God. And when they understand it, they quickly desire it and receive it! I have been blessed to help many Christians—even sometimes almost entire church congregations—receive the baptism in the Holy Spirit with speaking in tongues.

*The baptism in the Holy Spirit with speaking in tongues is a powerful key to your spiritual growth and personal breakthroughs* and should be greatly desired by every Christian. First Corinthians 12:31 (KJV) says:

*"³¹ But* **covet earnestly the best gifts**: *and yet shew I unto you a more excellent way."*

The New Kings James Version (NKJV) says:

*"³¹ But earnestly desire the best gifts…"*

This instructs us to *"covet earnestly the best gifts."* Normally we see the word "covet" in a negative sense, such as "do not covet," and most of the time we are commanded "do not covet." But here, we see that God is telling us that we *should* covet something. So, in spite of all the things we should *not* covet, there is something that we *should* covet.

What does that mean? The word *"covet"* means *"to burn with zeal, to be heated, or to boil; to* **desire earnestly** *and to* **pursue and strive after**; *and in a good sense, to be zealous in the pursuit of good."*

God tells us to *"covet earnestly the best gifts,"* or **"desire earnestly, pursue and strive after"** them, and this follows immediately after the teaching on the gifts, manifestations, and operations of the Holy Spirit in 1 Corinthians 12:1–11. God wants us to pursue the gifts, manifestations, and operations of the Holy Spirit. We are supposed to be seeking, coveting, desiring, and pursuing them! And they begin with the baptism in the Holy Spirit.

## There Are Three Baptisms

But what is the baptism in the Holy Spirit? First, we need to understand what baptism is. The Greek word used in the New Testament (the New Testament was written in Greek) for "baptism" is *"baptizo,"* which means *"to cover completely by immersion in something that envelops on all sides; to immerse; to submerge."*

We learn in Hebrews 6:1–2 that there is more than one baptism:

> *"1 Therefore let us leave the elementary teachings about Christ and go on to maturity, not laying again the foundation of repentance from acts that lead to death, and of faith in God, 2 **instruction about baptisms**, the laying on of hands, the resurrection of the dead, and eternal judgment."*

Notice it says in verse two, *"instruction about **baptisms**."* It does not say, *"baptism"* singular, but *"baptisms"* plural.

God is a triune (three-part) being and we are three-part beings—spirit, soul, and body. First Thessalonians 5:23 says:

> *"23 May God himself, the God of peace, sanctify you through and through. May your whole **spirit, soul and body** be kept blameless at the coming of our Lord Jesus Christ."*

Why, then, wouldn't there be three baptisms?

## Baptized Into Christ

The first baptism is when a person receives salvation and is born again[1]. At that time, he/she is *"baptized into Christ."* Many Christians have not heard of this, but it is described in Galatians 3:26–27:

> *"[26] You are all sons of God through faith in Christ Jesus, [27] for all of you who were **baptized into Christ** have clothed yourselves with Christ."*

We are born again[1] through faith alone, not of works, including any other form of baptism. This is clearly stated in Ephesians 2:8–9:

> *"[8] For it is by grace you have been saved, **through faith**—and this not from yourselves, it is the gift of God— [9] **not by works, so that no one can boast.**"*

Anyone who thinks they are saved by water baptism, going to church, good works, giving money, or any other action is mistaken.

When we receive Jesus as our Savior by faith, we are born again[1], and we are *"baptized into Christ"* and clothe ourselves with Christ. We become one with Him—He is the head and we are the body. John 14:20 says:

> *"[20] On that day you will realize that I am in my Father, and you are in me, and I am in you."*

4

Ephesians 5:23 says:

> *"23 For the husband is the head of the wife as* **Christ is the head of the church, his body,** *of which he is the Savior."*

And Colossians 1:18 says:

> *"18 And he is the head of the body, the church;"*

The only baptism required to go to heaven is being baptized into Christ, which the Holy Spirit does when you are born again. This has to be true because if a person calls on the Name of the Lord when he is dying, he will be saved and go to heaven even if he didn't get baptized in water or in the Holy Spirit, as it says in Romans 10:13:

> *"13 for, 'Everyone who calls on the name of the Lord will be saved.'"*

The only thing a person needs to do to be born again is receive Jesus Christ as their personal Savior by faith[1].

## Water Baptism

After a person is born again, they are encouraged to be water baptized. Matthew 28:19 says:

> *"19 Therefore go and make disciples of all nations,* **baptizing them in the name of the Father and of the Son and of the Holy Spirit,"**

This is referring to water baptism. We see many examples in the New Testament of water baptism. John the Baptist baptized many people in the Jordan River, and Jesus himself was water baptized by John (Matthew 3:13–17). Those who accepted Peter's message on the Day of Pentecost were water baptized (Acts 2:41), the converts in Samaria were water baptized when they believed Philip (Acts 8:12), the Ethiopian eunuch was baptized in water by Philip (Acts 8:36–38), the Apostle Paul was water baptized (Acts 9:18), and the Philippian jailer was water baptized by Paul and Silas after he believed on the Lord Jesus (Acts 16:30–34). Water baptism was a high priority to the Early Church, and therefore it should also be a priority in the lives of believers today.

Why should a Christian be baptized in water? Water baptism is a memorial in a person's life that should mark his thinking forever.

> ➢ It separates a believer's new life in Christ from his past life of sin.
> ➢ It is a foundation in a believer's new walk in Christ Jesus.
> ➢ It is the beginning of the renewing of the mind.
> ➢ It is a place where you forget the past.
> ➢ It is a funeral service to bury the old man and a resurrection site for the new man.
> ➢ It is an outward demonstration of the inward working of God in a believer's life.

➤ It is a public testimony before heaven, earth, and hell of a believer's faith in Jesus Christ and new birth.

And finally, being baptized *"in the name of"* Jesus Christ or the Father, the Son, and the Holy Spirit signifies a solemn confession of commitment, devotion, and service to that Name.

Some churches sprinkle babies with water and call it baptism, but if they understood Greek, they would understand that *"baptize"* means *"to submerge; to immerse and cover completely on all sides."* Therefore, sprinkling with water does not fulfill the definition of "baptism." Sprinkling can be a baby dedication unto God, but not baptism. By definition then, water baptism means to submerge completely under the water. Also, water baptism should be by faith and by choice of the one being baptized. In the case of baby sprinkling, the baby is not the one choosing to be baptized nor are they using their own personal faith.

Once you are born again and baptized into Christ through faith, it doesn't matter if you are baptized in the Holy Spirit next or baptized in water. At Cornelius' house, they were baptized in the Holy Spirit before they were baptized in water (Acts 10:34–48).

## What Is the Baptism in the Holy Spirit?

Now that we understand what baptism means, we can understand that baptism in the Holy Spirit means immersion in the Holy Spirit. It is when the Holy Spirit comes *upon* you and covers you completely. It is a baptism as real as water baptism, and it is a second experience in the Holy Spirit *after* you get born again.

Many Christians and some church denominations don't believe in this second experience. They believe you receive all of the Holy Spirit you can get when you are born again, and that's all there is. But there's more! And although you can get saved *and* immediately get baptized in the Holy Spirit (if you are ready to receive it—this doesn't happen often), **salvation does not automatically make you baptized in the Holy Spirit**. The baptism in the Holy Spirit is a second additional experience in the Holy Spirit after salvation.

## *In* You, Then *Upon* You

When you are born again by receiving Jesus Christ as your Savior, you are born *of the Spirit* as Jesus said in John 3:3–6:

> *"3 In reply Jesus declared, 'I tell you the truth, no one can see the kingdom of God unless he is born again.' 4 'How can a man be born when he is old?' Nicodemus asked. 'Surely he cannot enter a second time into his mother's womb to be born!' 5 Jesus*

> *answered, 'I tell you the truth, no one can enter the kingdom of God unless he is born of water and the Spirit. ⁶ Flesh gives birth to flesh, but the Spirit gives birth to spirit.'"*

When you are born again, the Holy Spirit comes to live *inside* of you. John 14:16–17 say:

> *"¹⁶ And I will ask the Father, and he will give you another Counselor to be with you forever— ¹⁷ the Spirit of truth. The world cannot accept him, because it neither sees him nor knows him. But you know him, for he lives with you and will be **in** you."*

When you are born again, the Holy Spirit lives *in* you. Some people who don't have the baptism in the Holy Spirit argue by saying, "But I already have the Holy Spirit." Yes, you have the Holy Spirit *in* you if you are born again. Absolutely correct. But there is something more that is available to every Christian than the Holy Spirit just being *in* you. There is also the baptism in the Holy Spirit in which the Holy Spirit comes *upon* you. We see that word specifically used in Acts 1:8 (NAB):

> *"⁸ But you will receive power when the holy Spirit comes **upon** you, and you will be my witnesses in Jerusalem, throughout Judea and Samaria, and to the ends of the earth."*

So we see in John 14:17 the Holy Spirit will be **in** you, but in Acts 1:8 the Holy Spirit will be **upon** you.

9

Those are two different things. They are not the same. If you remember in the book of Acts chapter two, when the Day of Pentecost had fully come, they were all together in one accord. Verse three says they saw what seemed to be tongues of fire that separated and came and sat **on** each of them.

Acts 2:1–4 (NKJV):

*"1 When the Day of Pentecost had fully come, they were all with one accord in one place. 2 And suddenly there came a sound from heaven, as of a rushing mighty wind, and it filled the whole house where they were sitting. 3 Then there appeared to them divided tongues, as of fire, and one sat **upon** each of them. 4 And they were all filled with the Holy Spirit and began to speak with other tongues, as the Spirit gave them utterance."*

On the Day of Pentecost, the Holy Spirit came and sat **upon** them and covered them completely on all sides. That was the baptism in the Holy Spirit.

## Two Experiences

In the New Testament, every person specifically mentioned who received the baptism in the Holy Spirit had already been born again previously! So, the New Testament specifically reveals they had two separate experiences at two different times with the Holy Spirit (actually, they had more than two experiences with the

Holy Spirit because they continued to have subsequent "baptisms" or infillings of the Holy Spirit repeatedly).

## The Twelve Disciples

The first example is the twelve disciples themselves. After Jesus' resurrection, John 20:1 says:

> *"¹ Early on the **first** day of the week, while it was still dark, Mary Magdalene went to the tomb and saw that the stone had been removed from the entrance."*

What day was it? It was the *first* day of the week. So it was immediately after Jesus' resurrection. On the evening of the *same day*, the twelve disciples were in the upper room with the doors locked for fear of the Jews. John 20:19–22 say:

> *"¹⁹ On the evening of that **first** day of the week [the same day], when the disciples were together, with the doors locked for fear of the Jews, Jesus came and stood among them and said, 'Peace be with you!' ²⁰ After he said this, he showed them his hands and side. The disciples were overjoyed when they saw the Lord. ²¹ Again Jesus said, 'Peace be with you! As the Father has sent me, I am sending you.' ²² And with that **he breathed on them and said, 'Receive the Holy Spirit.'"***

Jesus came and stood among them even though the doors were closed and locked. How did he do it?

11

He must have passed through the wall or he just suddenly appeared because he was in his glorified body. He came and stood among them and *"breathed on them and said, 'Receive the Holy Spirit.'"*

Many people have wondered what that experience was. Was that salvation, or was it the baptism in the Holy Spirit? It was salvation, the new birth of those disciples, because Jesus *"breathed on them."* In order to understand that, we need to go back to Genesis 2:7:

> *"7 the LORD God formed the man from the dust of the ground and **breathed into his nostrils the breath of life**, and the man became a living being."*

God formed the man from the dust of the ground, and then He breathed in him the breath of life, and the man became a living being. So what we see in John 20:22 is exactly what God did in Genesis 2:7. God breathed into Adam, and Adam became a living being, and four thousand years later, Jesus breathed on the disciples. What was that? It was the breath of life! And because we know they already had physical life, it was *spiritual life*, the *zoe* life of God. They needed spiritual life because sin had made the human race spiritually dead (Romans 5:12; 7:11,13), which is being disconnected from God[2].

Ephesians 2:1,4–5 say:

> *"1 As for you, **you were dead** in your transgressions and sins, ...4 But because of his great love*

12

> *for us, God, who is rich in mercy, [5]* **made us alive** *with Christ even when we were dead in transgressions—it is by grace you have been saved."*

So when Jesus breathed the breath of life into them, they became living beings *spiritually*. That word *"breathed"* is the key to understanding what happened to them. They became spiritually alive at that moment. So what was that experience? It was the new birth—they were born again!

Now we know they were born again in John 20. Just two chapters later, in Acts 1, you see Jesus stayed with the disciples for forty days after his resurrection before he ascended into heaven. And during that time he was teaching them. Acts 1:1–5 say:

> *"[1] In my former book, Theophilus, I wrote about all that Jesus began to do and to teach [2] until the day he was taken up to heaven, after giving instructions through the Holy Spirit* **to the apostles** *he had chosen. [3] After his suffering, he showed himself to these men and gave many convincing proofs that he was alive. He appeared to them over a period of forty days and spoke about the kingdom of God. [4] On one occasion, while he was eating with them, he gave them this command: 'Do not leave Jerusalem, but* **wait for the gift** *my Father promised, which you have heard me speak about. [5] For John baptized with water, but in a few days* **you will be baptized with the Holy Spirit.**'"

Jesus said, *"you **will be** baptized."* Who was the *"you"* he was talking to? It was the same disciples that were in the upper room in John 20. It was not a different group. These were not different disciples. So, to the same disciples that he breathed the breath of life on in John 20, forty days later he said, *"You **will be** baptized in the Holy Spirit."*

Then Acts 2:1–4 (NKJV) say:

> *"1 When the Day of Pentecost had fully come, they were all with one accord in one place. 2 And suddenly there came a sound from heaven, as of a rushing mighty wind, and it filled the whole house where they were sitting. 3 Then there appeared to them divided tongues, as of fire, and one sat upon each of them.* *4 **And they were all filled with the Holy Spirit and began to speak with other tongues,** as the Spirit gave them utterance."*

We have evidence here of a subsequent second experience in the Holy Spirit given to the Apostles. In John 20, they were born again, and fifty days later *("pente"* means *"fifty,"* so it was fifty days after Jesus' resurrection), on the Day of Pentecost, they were baptized in the Holy Spirit. So we see they had *two* experiences (and later, even more).

## The Converts in Samaria

Some people might say, "Well, that was because the Day of Pentecost had not yet come." All right, I will show you another example *after* the Day of Pentecost of people having two separate experiences—first being born again and later being baptized in the Holy Spirit *with* the evidence of speaking in tongues.

In Acts 8:5–6, we see the believers in Samaria, and it says:

> *"5 Philip went down to a city in Samaria and proclaimed the Christ there. 6 When the crowds heard Philip and saw the miraculous signs he did, they all paid close attention to what he said."*

Verse 12 says:

> *"12 But when they **believed** Philip as he preached the good news of the kingdom of God and the name of Jesus Christ, they were **baptized**, both men and women."*

They believed and were baptized. What does that mean? ***They were born again*** when they believed the gospel that Phillip preached (Phillip was an evangelist). How do you get born again[1]? Acts 16:30–31 say:

> *"30 He [the Philippian jailer] then brought them out and asked, 'Sirs, what must I do to be saved?' 31 They replied, '**Believe in the Lord Jesus**, and you will be saved—you and your household.'"*

So we know these Samaritans got born again through Philip's ministry.

Now, go down to Acts 8:14–15:

> *"14 When the apostles in Jerusalem heard that Samaria had accepted the word of God, they sent Peter and John to them. 15 When they arrived, they prayed for them that they might receive the Holy Spirit,"*

Verse 15 says:

> *"15 When they arrived, they prayed for them that they might* **receive the Holy Spirit***."*

But wait a minute. They already had the Holy Spirit when they believed Philip, didn't they? Yes, they had the Holy Spirit in the new birth, but this is talking about the baptism in the Holy Spirit.

Let's keep reading. Acts 8:15–16:

> *"15 When they arrived, they prayed for them that they might receive the Holy Spirit, 16 because the Holy Spirit had not yet come* **upon** *any of them;…"*

Upon, upon, upon. That is the key word of the baptism in the Holy Spirit.

> *"16 because the Holy Spirit had not yet come* **upon** *any of them; they had simply been baptized* **into** *the name of the Lord Jesus."*

And verse 17 says:

> *"¹⁷ Then Peter and John placed their hands on them,*
> **and they received the Holy Spirit."**

So they had a second experience in the Holy Spirit *after* they were born again. They were born again under the ministry of Philip, and they were baptized in the Holy Spirit under the ministry of Peter and John. So we see again there were two separate experiences in the Holy Spirit.

## The Converts in Ephesus

A third example is the converts in Ephesus. Acts 19:1–7 say:

> *"¹ While Apollos was at Corinth, Paul took the road through the interior and arrived at Ephesus. There he found some disciples ² and asked them, 'Did you receive the Holy Spirit when you believed?' They answered, 'No, we have not even heard that there is a Holy Spirit.' ³ So Paul asked, 'Then what baptism did you receive?' 'John's baptism,' they replied. ⁴ Paul said, 'John's baptism was a baptism of repentance. He told the people to believe in the one coming after him, that is, in Jesus.' ⁵ On hearing this, they were baptized into the name of the Lord Jesus. ⁶ When Paul placed his hands on them, the Holy Spirit came on them, and they spoke in tongues and prophesied. ⁷ There were about twelve men in all."*

Here again we see that these men first were born again. In verse one, Paul said, *"when you believed."* Verses three and four show they had received the baptism of repentance. Verse five says:

> *"⁵ On hearing this, they were baptized into the name of the Lord Jesus."*

This shows they were born again.

After that,

> *"⁶ When Paul placed his hands on them, the Holy Spirit came **on** them, and they spoke in tongues and prophesied."*

So again, we see that they were baptized in the Holy Spirit *after* they were born again when the Holy Spirit came **on** or **upon** them, and they **all** spoke in tongues.

## The Baptism in the Holy Spirit Brings the Power of God Into Our Lives

The baptism in the Holy Spirit brings the power of God into our lives because the Holy Spirit **is** the power of God. The baptism in the Holy Spirit is being *"endued [clothed] with power from on high"* because it is being clothed with the Holy Spirit, who **is** the power of God. In Luke 24:49, Jesus said:

*"⁴⁹ I am going to send you what my Father has promised; but stay in the city until you have been* **clothed** [KJV – *endued*] **with power from on high."'**

Clothed with power! There's a clothing of power when you receive the baptism in the Holy Spirit! Praise God!

Acts 1:8 says:

*"⁸ But you will* **receive power** *when the Holy Spirit comes* **on** *you..."*

Have you ever thought, "I feel so powerless?" That's because you need the baptism in the Holy Spirit! There is a supernatural power given to believers after they are born again when they are baptized in the Holy Spirit, and it is very necessary! If Christians would just understand the added power that comes into their lives when they are baptized in the Holy Spirit, every Christian would desire it!

This power is for ourselves personally, but it is also power to be witnesses for Jesus.

Let's keep reading Acts 1:8:

*"⁸ But you will* **receive power** *when the Holy Spirit comes* **on** *you;* **and you will be my witnesses** *in Jerusalem, and in all Judea and Samaria, and to the ends of the earth."*

This power from the Holy Spirit to be His witness is so necessary that Jesus basically said, "Don't leave home without it!"

Luke 24:47–49 say:

> *"⁴⁷ 'and **repentance and forgiveness of sins will be preached in his name to all nations, beginning at Jerusalem.** ⁴⁸ **You are witnesses** of these things. ⁴⁹ I am going to send you what my Father has promised; **but stay in the city until you have been clothed with power from on high.**'"*

Jesus said, "Go, but wait!"

In Acts 1, when Jesus appeared to his disciples for forty days, he again told them to *wait for the power*. Acts 1:3–5 say:

> *"³ After his suffering, he showed himself to these men and gave many convincing proofs that he was alive. He appeared to them over a period of forty days and spoke about the kingdom of God. ⁴ On one occasion, while he was eating with them, he gave them this command: **Do not leave Jerusalem, but wait** for the gift my Father promised, which you have heard me speak about. ⁵ For John baptized with water, but in a few days you will be baptized with the Holy Spirit.'"*

Remember, this was *after* they were born again, because they were born again on the same day Jesus was resurrected from the dead.

During these forty days after His resurrection, Jesus gave the disciples the Great Commission:

> *"15 Go into all the world and preach the gospel to every creature"* (Mark 16:15 NKJV).

and

> *"19 Therefore go and make disciples of all nations, baptizing them in the name of the Father and of the Son and of the Holy Spirit"* (Matthew 28:19).

But then he said in Acts 1:4–5, **"Do not leave Jerusalem, but wait:"**

> **"4 Do not leave Jerusalem, but wait for the gift my Father promised,** *which you have heard me speak about.* **5** *For John baptized with water, but in a few days you will be* **baptized with the Holy Spirit."**

Jesus was saying, **"Go, but wait.** Don't go yet. Hold your horses! Don't go without the power! Wait in Jerusalem until you get the power, and then go." So he was telling them, "You will need this power even to be a witness in all the world."

There is a power available to you as a born-again child of God to live your life and to be a witness for Jesus Christ, and it comes in the baptism in the Holy Spirit! Don't leave home without it!

# Chapter Two

# What Is Tongues?

N ow then, what is tongues? The word *"tongue"* simply means *"language."* New Testament tongues is a *supernatural* gift from the Holy Spirit by which a person speaks a language they do not know. Some people argue against the gifts of the Spirit trying to make them a mere natural human ability, removing the supernatural element of the gifts of the Spirit. As such, they say that the "gift of tongues" is just somebody who can speak more than one language. That is not correct. *All* of the gifts of the Spirit are *supernatural* gifts imparted by the Holy Spirit that are beyond a person's natural ability.

First Corinthians 13:1 says:

*"¹ If I speak in the tongues of men and of angels..."*

We see here that there are both heavenly languages and earthly languages, and speaking in tongues is speaking in either a heavenly or earthly language that

God gives you to speak that you haven't learned—one that you do not know with your natural understanding and you will never learn. If it is a language spoken somewhere else on earth, someone else may know it, but you will never know it. Thus, it is given to you to speak by the Holy Spirit.

We see this in Acts 2:4–11:

> *"⁴ All of them were filled with the Holy Spirit and began to speak in other tongues as the Spirit enabled them. ⁵ Now there were staying in Jerusalem God-fearing Jews from every nation under heaven. ⁶ When they heard this sound, a crowd came together in bewilderment, because each one heard them speaking in his own language. ⁷ Utterly amazed, they asked: 'Are not all these men who are speaking Galileans? ⁸ Then how is it that each of us hears them in his own native language? ⁹ Parthians, Medes and Elamites; residents of Mesopotamia, Judea and Cappadocia, Pontus and Asia, ¹⁰ Phrygia and Pamphylia, Egypt and the parts of Libya near Cyrene; visitors from Rome ¹¹ (both Jews and converts to Judaism); Cretans and Arabs—we hear them declaring the wonders of God in our own tongues!'"*

I have heard of modern testimonies of this happening. For example, Brother Hagin said he was praying in tongues during a service one time and a man came to him after the service and said, "You were speaking perfect Greek." Well, Brother Hagin never learned Greek. He did not know what he was saying, but the other man did.

Another testimony I heard was about a missionary to East Asia. He preached about the baptism in the Holy Spirit and speaking in tongues, and then after the service, he had an altar call for people to come forward to receive the baptism in the Holy Spirit. He passed one woman who was speaking in English after he laid hands on her, and he told her, "Sister, now stop speaking in English and start speaking in tongues, an unknown language." The pastor of the church said to him, "Brother, she doesn't speak English." So she was speaking in English by the Holy Spirit because she had never learned English!

Another story is about an evangelist who was traveling across Europe I believe, and he was directed by the Holy Spirit to get off the train at a depot in a country not his own. When he did, he spotted two men and was led by the Holy Spirit to go speak to them. But he did not speak the local language, so he began speaking in tongues by the Holy Spirit. When he did, he saw that they understood what he was saying. When he stopped, they spoke, and then he spoke again in tongues. Then they bowed their heads and began speaking like they were praying. He knew they were receiving the Lord Jesus as their Savior and being born again! Praise God!

A similar testimony was about a missionary to Africa, and he went to a village where he did not have an interpreter. But as he spoke in tongues, they responded, and he could see they were receiving the Lord Jesus as their Savior.

This is a supernatural gift of the Holy Spirit that is one of the *ministry* gifts (1 Cor. 12:4–11). It is as the Holy Spirit wills, not as we desire or choose, unlike our personal prayer and praise language that God gives us which we can speak all day every day (I will explain more about this difference in a moment).

So there can be times when you may speak an earthly language by the Holy Spirit, and you don't know you're speaking an earthly language, and you don't know what you're saying but someone else may. However, this supernatural gift will never be a language that you have learned.

When it is a heavenly tongue, it is a secret language spoken between you and God that the devil himself cannot understand! That's some great code talk! And boy, does it frustrate the devil!

## Two Categories of the Gift of Tongues: Private & Public

Something that many Christians don't understand (and it is one of the hindrances to them receiving) is that there are two categories of the gift of tongues: private or personal tongues and public or ministry tongues. They have different purposes and are used at different times. Some Christians argue against speaking in tongues because they don't understand the two categories, and they are trying to apply the rules for public tongues to private tongues.

Private or personal tongues is personal communication with God, as it says in First Corinthians 14:2:

> *"² For anyone who speaks in a tongue does not speak to men but to God."*

It is you talking to God and God talking to you. It includes prayer, praise, and worship, and it includes your spirit fellowshipping with the Holy Spirit (we will get into these in detail later).

Public tongues is God speaking through a person to other people. It's a *"ministry"* of tongues. As I exampled previously, some ministers have spoken in a tongue that was unknown to them while it was known to hearers, which led the hearers to receive Jesus as their personal Savior. In these cases, their speaking in tongues was a ministry.

Public tongues is a type of prophecy because it is God speaking to people.

## Wrong Idea #1: "Do All Speak in Tongues?"

One of the arguments that Christians have brought against speaking in tongues is based on 1 Corinthians 12:30.

First Corinthians 12:28–31 say:

> *"28 And in the church God has appointed first of all apostles, second prophets, third teachers, then workers of miracles, also those having gifts of healing, those able to help others, those with gifts of administration, and those speaking in different kinds of tongues. 29 Are all apostles? Are all prophets? Are all teachers? Do all work miracles? 30 Do all have gifts of healing?* **Do all speak in tongues?** *Do all interpret? 31 But eagerly desire the greater gifts. And now I will show you the most excellent way."*

Based on this verse, these Christians say that not all Christians will speak in tongues. What they don't understand is that this passage is talking about *ministry* gifts. It asks, *"Are all apostles? Are all prophets? Are all teachers?"* So this question, *"Do all speak in tongues?"* is directly pertaining to the *public ministry* gift of speaking in tongues. The answer is no, not all Christians have the ministry gift of speaking in tongues, which is *"God speaking through a person to other people."*

But because personal tongues is personal communication with God—it is you talking to God

28

and God talking to you, including prayer, praise and worship, and your spirit fellowshipping with the Holy Spirit—**should all Christians pray? Should all Christians praise and worship God? Should all Christians fellowship with the Holy Spirit?** *Absolutely yes!* Therefore, the personal, private gift of tongues *is for EVERY born-again Christian!*

## Wrong Idea #2: There Must Always Be an Interpretation

Another wrong idea people have is that when someone speaks in tongues, there must always be an interpretation. This is also incorrect based upon the two categories of tongues. When it is personal tongues—you talking to God—*it does not require an interpretation* **because God understands what you're saying!**

But when it is the public ministry of tongues— God speaking to people—yes, there must be an interpretation because you are talking to people who don't understand what you're saying unless you are speaking by the Holy Spirit a language they know, such as I have previously exampled.

First Corinthians 14:2–4 say:

*"2 For anyone who speaks in a tongue does not speak to men but to God. Indeed, no one understands him; he utters mysteries with his spirit. 3 But everyone who prophesies speaks to men for their strengthening,*

*encouragement and comfort. <sup>4</sup> He who speaks in a tongue edifies himself, but he who prophesies edifies the church."*

In this passage, although it is somewhat unclear, Paul is comparing personal tongues to the public ministry gift of tongues. In verse two, he is talking about speaking to God; in verse three, he is talking about speaking to people; and in verse four, he is talking about both.

First Corinthians 14:5 says:

*"<sup>5</sup> ...He who prophesies is greater than one who speaks in tongues, unless he interprets, so that the church may be edified."*

This shows us that **tongues with interpretation is equal to prophecy.**

So in regard to ministry to the church, tongues must be interpreted in order for the people to be *"edified, strengthened, encouraged, and comforted"* (which is the purpose of prophecy—verses 3 and 4), unless they already have knowledge of the language spoken in a tongue.

## What About Corporate Tongues?

Another question people ask is, can people pray and worship in tongues corporately at the same time? Yes. Just like you can pray and worship at the same time corporately with other Christians in your known language, you can pray and worship in tongues corporately—and that without interpretation because each one is still *speaking directly to God, and He understands!*

## How Can You Speak in a Language You Don't Know?

You say, "Well, how can I say something that I don't understand?" It's easy. Let me show you. Say this: *"käpingä"* (pronounced like *cop-ing-ah*). Then say *"köht"* (pronounced like *coat*). Now say, *"käpingä köht."* Do you know the meaning of what you said? Probably not. That is the Pohnpeian language spoken on a little island called Pohnpei in Micronesia in the middle of the Pacific Ocean. It means *"praise God."* So you just praised God in a language you did not understand!

How did you do it? I taught you. I taught you what to say without telling you first what it means. After you said it, I explained to you what it means. And when you first said it, you had to trust me, right? You might have thought, "Cherri, you better not be making me say cuss words." No, I wasn't, and you trusted me (if you said it).

In the same way, you trust the Holy Spirit and say what He prompts you to say from within your spirit. You trust Him that they are good and *real* words. *It requires faith*, and that is the bottom line. When you speak in tongues, you have to speak by faith. You trust

God as you get promptings by the Holy Spirit from within you to say sounds that don't make any sense to you. They're goofy. They're strange. Why? Because you don't know what they mean. They will always sound strange to you because you don't know what they mean, just like "käpingä kōht" sounds strange to you.

I'll tell you another one that sounds strange to us. (This is the phonetic spelling, not the actual spelling.) Say "nay noo nee noo pray me stoo nah noo" (actual spelling – Nenu ninnu premistunaanu). That is Telugu, a language spoken in Andhra Pradesh, India, and it means *"I love you."*

I like that one because it sounds so funny. It almost sounds like Mork from Ork (that dates me!). Notice that if you said those words, you trusted me to say things when you didn't know what they mean. And they do sound funny to your ears because they are unfamiliar to you and you don't know what they mean.

## God Doesn't Make You

Notice something else. ***I taught you what to say, but I did not make you say it***. I did not force you. I did not open your mouth and wiggle your tongue and take control of you to make you speak. I had no physical control over you. I simply taught you what to say, and you said it by your own choice and power. That is *exactly* what the Holy Spirit does! He teaches you *what* to say, but He doesn't make you say it.

I've helped people receive the baptism in the Holy Spirit in almost every country that I've gone to. I've seen almost entire church congregations receive the baptism in the Holy Spirit. I've also had people tell me, "I've been seeking this for ten years, and I finally got it tonight. It was so easy."

The reason they hadn't received it for ten years was not because God was waiting to give it to them but because they didn't understand how easy it is to receive it and start speaking in tongues. A lot of people have a misunderstanding that the power of God takes over and controls you and makes you speak in tongues—that He actually manipulates your mouth to speak. No, absolutely not. God is not a manipulator—God is not a controller. You are not a puppet on a string. You have a free will. You are a free agent.

If you are waiting for God to come on you and make you speak in tongues, *it will never happen*. His anointing can come on you and prompt you to speak, but He will *never* make you. That's why many Christians do not speak in tongues—because they say, "Well, if God wants me to speak in tongues, He'll make me." No, He won't. He offers you the gift, but the only thing God will do is prompt and teach you, and then you must willingly follow and start speaking *by faith* what He gives you.

When you get the stirrings down on the inside of you to say strange sounds, you need to say them, because you have to *yield* to the Holy Spirit—follow His leading and promptings. He will not control you. You simply respond to Him by following those promptings in your spirit to say sounds that don't even sound like words to you.

## Start Like a Baby

When you first start speaking in tongues, oftentimes the words don't sound like words. They sound like simple, repeated syllables because it is just like a baby learning to speak. Usually, a baby's first word is "Mama" or "Dada" or "Papa." Well, what is that? That is one sound or syllable repeated over and over: "Mama" is one syllable repeated, and "Papa" is one syllable repeated (it's even the same in other languages). If you repeat them over and over, it's "Mama, Mama, Mama, Mama, Papa, Papa, Papa, Papa." This is a common way people begin. Occasionally, people start with a fluent, developed language, but many times people start speaking in tongues like a baby learning to talk.

Isaiah 28:11 (KJV) says:

*"11 For with stammering lips and another tongue will he speak to this people."*

This is in the Old Testament. Isaiah prophesied about speaking in tongues in the Old Testament! Isaiah said it sounds like stammering lips, or we might say a stuttering tongue, and sometimes it does sound like stuttering like "mama mama papa papa." It might be "ba ba ba ba da da da da na na na na." That sounds like stuttering, and that could be the way you start. Don't be afraid of a stuttering tongue. *If you are willing to speak that out, it will begin to flow like a river*, like it says in John 7:38–39:

> *"38 Whoever believes in me, as the Scripture has said, streams of living water will flow from within him.' 39 By this he meant the Spirit…"*

As you continue speaking in tongues, it will grow from a trickle to a stream and then to a river! You will get more and more words and utterance, and it will grow and develop into a full, fluent language.

## Be *Being* Filled

As we read earlier in Acts 2:4, the baptism in the Holy Spirit is also called being "filled with the Holy Spirit":

> *"4 All of them were **filled with the Holy Spirit** and began to speak in other tongues as the Spirit enabled them."*

Ephesians 5:18 says:

> *"18 Do not get drunk on wine, which leads to debauchery. Instead, **be filled with the Spirit.**"*

The words *"be filled"* in the original Greek text is a continuous action verb. So literally translated, it reads, *"Be [**being** or **continually be**] filled with the Spirit."*

The Complete Jewish Bible (CJB) says, ***"keep on being filled with the Spirit."***

## The Disciples

We see that the disciples were "filled with the Spirit" on more than one occasion. After they were filled with the Holy Spirit in Acts 2, they were filled again in Acts 4. Acts 4:29–31 say:

> *"29 Now, Lord, consider their threats and enable your servants to speak your word with great boldness. 30 Stretch out your hand to heal and perform miraculous signs and wonders through the name of your holy servant Jesus.' 31 After they prayed, the place where they were meeting was shaken. **And they were all filled with the Holy Spirit** and spoke the word of God boldly."*

## The Apostle Paul

After his conversion on the road to Damascus, Paul was filled with the Holy Spirit first in Acts 9:17:

> *"17 Then Ananias went to the house and entered it. Placing his hands on Saul, he said, "**Brother** Saul, the Lord—Jesus, who appeared to you on the road as*

*you were coming here—has sent me so that you may see again and **be filled with the Holy Spirit.**"*

Notice, he was "filled with the Spirit" *after* his conversion on the road to Damascus—again, the new birth and the infilling (baptism) of the Holy Spirit were two separate experiences.

Then in Acts 13:52 it says he was "filled with the Holy Spirit" again:

*"52 And the disciples [Paul and Barnabas] were **filled** with joy and **with the Holy Spirit.**"*

In 1 Corinthians 14:18, Paul said:

*"18 I thank God that I speak in tongues more than all of you."*

First of all, he expected *all* of them to speak in tongues, and he did it more than *all* of them (we again see that *every* believer should speak in tongues). Obviously, this means he frequently spoke in tongues. If he did it more than *all* of them, it was probably throughout the day every day!

A pastor, who argued about not needing the baptism in the Holy Spirit, said to me one time, "Well, I knew a Pentecostal preacher who committed adultery. Being filled with the Holy Spirit didn't cause him to live holy." My answer to that is, he wasn't filled with the Holy Spirit that day! And he probably hadn't been filled with the Holy Spirit for many days, weeks, months, and possibly years!

Just because a person is baptized in the Holy Spirit—also called being "filled with the Holy Spirit"—one day, *doesn't mean they are filled with the Holy Spirit permanently from then on.* (It doesn't mean they lose their salvation. It just means they are not *full* of the Holy Spirit.) No. ***Just like we need the Word of God every day, we also need to be filled with the Holy Spirit every day!*** That's why Ephesians 5:18 says:

> *"18 Do not get drunk on wine, which leads to debauchery. Instead,* **be [being] filled [keep on being filled;** *or* **continually be filled] with the Spirit."**

# Chapter Three

# 23 Reasons Why Every Believer Should Speak in Tongues

There are *many* reasons why every believer should speak in tongues! As you study this, it should stir you up to desire speaking in tongues regularly and frequently. It is something you should do every day. Just like you pray every day, you should also pray in tongues every day. Here are some powerful reasons why every believer should speak in tongues.

## #1 Tongues Is the Initial Sign of the Baptism in the Holy Spirit

Number one, tongues is the initial sign of the baptism in the Holy Spirit. There are other signs, and you can receive other gifts after you have received the baptism in the Holy Spirit, but the first sign and evidence that you have received the baptism in the Holy Spirit is that you speak in other tongues. Why can I say it's the first sign or evidence?

Well first, let me give you an example. When you're born again, you receive the Holy Spirit *in* you. But nobody can see Him, right? You can be sitting in your chair while I'm talking, and you can quietly—in your heart—raise a prayer to God without speaking out loud, without moving your lips, and say, "Lord Jesus, come into my heart. Forgive me of my sins. Be my Savior. I give you my life." You just sit there with your lips closed making a silent prayer, and I don't see or know anything has happened to you because most of the time, the moment a person is saved, there is no outward evidence because it's something that happens on the *inside*. But baptism is *outward*.

Let's go back to the definition of baptism. It is immersion in something that *covers* on all sides. If we consider water baptism, for example, when a person is baptized in water, is there visible evidence that other people around can see that they've been water baptized? Absolutely! They're dripping with water! It's a visible sign for other people to see. They got wet. They got baptized. The water is visibly *upon* them. It's the same with the baptism in the Holy Spirit.

## The Day of Pentecost

Let's look at scripture. *Speaking in other tongues was the first visible, outward sign of the baptism in the Holy Spirit in the book of Acts,* and it came immediately when the disciples were baptized in the Holy Spirit on the Day of Pentecost.

Acts 2:1–4 say:

> *"¹ When the day of Pentecost came, they were all together in one place. ² Suddenly a sound like the blowing of a violent wind came from heaven and filled the whole house where they were sitting. ³ They saw what seemed to be tongues of fire that separated and came to rest on each of them. ⁴* **All of them were filled with the Holy Spirit and began to speak in other tongues as the Spirit enabled them.** *"*

Notice in verse four, speaking in other tongues came *with* the infilling of the Holy Spirit, and not just some or a few of them spoke in tongues, but *all of them spoke in tongues!* This is proof that speaking in tongues is not just for a few Christians.

## The First Gentile Converts

Let me give you another scripture proof. In Acts 10, Peter was praying on the rooftop of the house where he was staying, and he saw a vision from God (see Acts 10:1–23). A sheet was lowered from heaven by its four corners, and in the sheet were all kinds of unclean animals. God said, "Arise and eat Peter." But Peter said, "Surely not Lord! I have never eaten anything unclean." God answered, "Do not call anything unclean that God has made clean."

Peter had this vision three times, and then after the vision finished and the sheet was taken back into heaven, some men came to the door of the house where he was staying. Then the Holy Spirit said to Peter, "I have sent these men. Go with them." So he went down from the rooftop and met the men who had come to the house and discovered they were Gentiles.

These men told Peter an angel had come to their master, Cornelius, a Roman centurion, and told him to have Peter come to his house. However, it was against Jewish law and custom for a Jew to enter the house of a Gentile or to even fellowship with a Gentile because Gentiles were considered unclean (thus the reason for the vision from heaven).

Acts 10 took place ten years after the Day of Pentecost, and up to that time, during those ten years, the disciples and other Jews who had been saved and baptized in the Holy Spirit had had no fellowship with Gentiles. So when the Holy Spirit told Peter to go with the Gentile men to a Gentile's home, it was a total break from custom and against Jewish law. So Peter had to have a word from God to break the Jewish law—he had to hear from God, or he would never have dared to break the Jewish law. Since the Holy Spirit told him to go, he went with the men to Cornelius' house, and he preached the gospel to them about Jesus Christ (see Acts 10:24–43).

While Peter was preaching to them about Jesus and forgiveness of sins, stating that *"everyone who believes in Him receives forgiveness of sins through his name"* (verse 43), Acts 10:44–46 say:

> *"⁴⁴ While Peter was still speaking these words, the Holy Spirit came **on all** who heard the message. ⁴⁵ The circumcised believers who had come with Peter **were astonished** that the gift of the Holy Spirit had been poured out even on the Gentiles. ⁴⁶ **For they heard them speaking in tongues** and praising God. Then Peter said, ⁴⁷ 'Can anyone keep these people from being baptized with water? They have received the Holy Spirit just as we have.'"*

Notice that the Jewish believers who went with Peter to Cornelius' house had never dreamed the Gentiles could be saved, let alone get baptized in the Holy Spirit! Surely not the Gentiles! But there was one convincing proof that the Gentiles had been saved and been baptized in the Holy Spirit—they spoke in other tongues! This was the convincing proof! And it was not just a few of them but *all* of them!

Peter then went back to Jerusalem, and the word had spread to Jerusalem that Peter had gone into a Gentile's house. Oh, no! God forbid! Then, the circumcised believers in Jerusalem, the Jewish Christians, put Peter on trial, saying essentially, "How dare you go into the house of a Gentile?" So Peter told the whole story about the vision of the sheet coming down from heaven. Acts 11:1–4 say:

*"¹ The apostles and the brothers throughout Judea heard that the Gentiles also had received the word of God. ² So when Peter went up to Jerusalem, the circumcised believers criticized him ³ and said, 'You went into the house of uncircumcised men and ate with them.' ⁴ Peter began and explained everything to them precisely as it had happened:"*

Then, in Acts 11:15–18, Peter said:

*"¹⁵ 'As I began to speak, the Holy Spirit came **on** them as he had come **on** us at the beginning. ¹⁶ Then I remembered what the Lord had said: 'John baptized with water, but you will be **baptized with the Holy Spirit.**' ¹⁷ **So if God gave them the same gift as he gave us, who believed in the Lord Jesus Christ, who was I to think that I could oppose God?'** ¹⁸ When they heard this, they had no further objections and praised God, saying, 'So then, God has granted even the Gentiles repentance unto life.'"*

Here we see the evidence that convinced the Jewish believers that Gentiles could not only be saved but also be baptized in the Holy Spirit was the evidence of speaking in tongues! **It was the convincing proof!** If speaking in tongues was the convincing proof to the Jewish believers that the Gentiles had also been baptized in the Holy Spirit, then it is also our convincing proof!

## Simon & the Converts in Samaria

Another example is Simon and the converts in Samaria. As we looked at in Acts 8, Philip preached the gospel in Samaria and the people were saved and water baptized (Acts 8:12). Then Peter and John came and they received the baptism in the Holy Spirit through the laying on of hands. We read in Acts 8:14–17:

*"14 When the apostles in Jerusalem heard that Samaria had accepted the word of God, they sent Peter and John to them. 15 When they arrived, they prayed for them that they might receive the Holy Spirit, 16 because the Holy Spirit had not yet come **upon** any of them; they had simply been baptized into the name of the Lord Jesus. 17 Then Peter and John placed their hands on them, and they received the Holy Spirit."*

But there was a man named Simon in Samaria who had been a sorcerer and had amazed the people. He also got born again. Acts 8:9,13 say:

*"9 Now for some time a man named Simon had practiced sorcery in the city and amazed all the people of Samaria. He boasted that he was someone great, 13 Simon himself believed and was baptized. And he followed Philip everywhere, astonished by the great signs and miracles he saw."*

Then Acts 8:17–20 say:

> *"17 Then Peter and John placed their hands on them, and they received the Holy Spirit. 18 When Simon **saw** that the Spirit was given at the laying on of the apostles' hands, he offered them money 19 and said, 'Give me also this ability so that everyone on whom I lay my hands may receive the Holy Spirit.' 20 Peter answered: 'May your money perish with you, because you thought you could buy the gift of God with money!'"*

The first point I want to show you is that you cannot "see" the new birth. You cannot "see" the Holy Spirit coming *into* a person. But Simon *"**saw** that the Spirit was given at the laying on of the apostles' hands,"* and as we mentioned earlier, they had already been born again under Philip's ministry, so this was the baptism in the Holy Spirit. So there had to be an outward, physical, visible evidence that Simon *saw*.

Then, look at verse 21 in the King James Version (KJV):

> *"21 Thou hast neither part nor lot in this **matter**: for thy heart is not right in the sight of God."*

The word *"matter"* in the Greek text is the word *"logos"* which means *"speech, spoken word, sayings; the act of speaking."* So literally translated, this verse reads:

> *"21 Thou hast neither part nor lot in this **speech; act of speaking**: for thy heart is not right in the sight of God."*

This reveals they were *speaking!* Peter called it a *"gift of God"* (verse 20). It was the gift of speaking in tongues! In comparing it to other scriptures, the only outward visible evidence of the Holy Spirit coming *upon* a person is speaking in other tongues!

Also, I want to point out that *all* of them received the Holy Spirit with outward, visible evidence. Simon said in verse 19:

> *"19 'Give me also this ability so that **everyone** on whom I lay my hands may receive the Holy Spirit.'"*

He obviously saw that *everyone* Peter and John laid hands on received the Holy Spirit (verse 17). This again is another scripture that proves *every* believer can and should speak in tongues!

## The Converts in Ephesus

One more scriptural confirmation that speaking in tongues comes immediately when people receive the baptism in the Holy Spirit is the converts in Ephesus. As we read earlier in Acts 19:6:

> *"6 When Paul placed his hands on them, the Holy Spirit came **on** them, **and they spoke in tongues** and prophesied."*

We have these four examples in the book of Acts that speaking in other tongues was the first visible, outward sign of the baptism in the Holy Spirit, and it came *immediately* when people were baptized in the Holy Spirit. Also, **every believer present received it**. So we know that speaking in tongues is the evidence of being baptized in the Holy Spirit, and **it is God's will for *every* believer!**

## #2 Speaking in Tongues Is the Entrance Into the Supernatural

Speaking in tongues is the entrance into the supernatural. Speaking in tongues is the entrance into the realm of the miraculous. Speaking in tongues is the entrance into the gifts of the Spirit that enables you to operate in other spiritual *ministry* gifts, such as working miracles, gifts of healing, tongues, and interpretation of tongues, discerning of spirits, etc. (1 Cor. 12:4–11). Those *ministry* gifts, manifestations, and operations of the Holy Spirit follow the *personal* gift of speaking in tongues, as the Holy Spirit wills. In other words, you have to receive the baptism in the Holy Spirit for yourself before you can operate in the *ministry* gifts of the Holy Spirit.

## #3 Speaking in Tongues Gives Thanks to God Beautifully

Another reason for speaking in tongues is because you *"give thanks well"* to God. First Corinthians 14:15–17 say:

> *"15 So what shall I do? I will pray with my spirit, but I will also pray with my mind [KJV – understanding]; I will sing with my spirit, but I will*

*also sing with my mind* [KJV – *understanding*]. *[16] If you are praising God with your spirit, how can one who finds himself among those who do not understand say 'Amen' to your **thanksgiving**, since he does not know what you are saying? [17] You may be **giving thanks well enough**, but the other man is not edified."*

Verse 16 says, *"how can one who finds himself among those who do not understand say 'Amen' to your **thanksgiving**,"* and verse 17 says, *"You may be **giving thanks well enough**."*

The word *"well"* in the Greek text means *"beautifully, finely, excellently."* So you could be praising and giving thanks to God when you speak in tongues, and if so, you are doing it "beautifully, finely, and excellently!" He loves to hear it!

Acts 2:11 says:

*"[11] ...we hear them declaring the wonders of God in our own tongues!"*

Speaking in tongues, therefore, magnifies God.

If there is praise and thankfulness in your heart, then it's praise coming out your mouth when you are speaking in tongues because Matthew 12:34 says:

*"[34] ...for out of the overflow of the heart the mouth speaks."*

## #4 Singing in Tongues Is the Quickest Way to Enter Into the Glory of God's Presence

Speaking and singing in tongues is ministering to yourself and to the Lord. It is one of the things Jesus meant when he talked about worshiping the Father in spirit and truth. John 4:23–24 say:

> *"23 Yet a time is coming and has now come when the true worshipers will* **worship the Father in spirit and truth,** *for they are the kind of worshipers the Father seeks. 24* [NKJV] *God is Spirit, and* **those who worship Him must worship in spirit and truth."**

Worshiping the Father *"in spirit and truth"* can be done both in our known language and in tongues, just as Paul said in 1 Corinthians 14:15:

> *"15 So what shall I do? I will pray with my spirit, but I will also pray with my mind* [KJV – *understanding*]; **I will sing with my spirit, but I will also sing with my mind** [KJV – *understanding*]."

Obviously, since Paul is contrasting singing with his spirit to singing with his understanding, it means that singing with his spirit is *not* singing with understanding, so that would be singing in tongues. When you sing in tongues, you can make up a melody or you can sing a familiar melody of a chorus you know but change the words to tongues.

It is so evident that when you sing in tongues—not just pray, but start singing in tongues—it catches you up quickly in the Spirit, in the anointing (not that you lose sense of where you are, but His presence and anointing become strong). You can immediately feel you are entering the presence of God. When you *pray* in tongues, you can get that connection in the Spirit, but it's sometimes more gradual and slower building the anointing. *Singing* in tongues is like a zip line right into the glory! I love to sing in tongues. It's so beautiful as you feel like you're caught up in the Spirit with the Lord!

## #5 Speaking in Tongues Brings Spiritual Edification & Strengthening

Speaking in tongues brings spiritual edification. First Corinthians 14:4 says:

*"⁴ He who speaks in a tongue edifies himself,"*

The New English Translation (NET) says:

*"⁴ The one who speaks in a tongue builds himself up"*

And the New Living Translation (NLT) says:

> *"⁴ A person who speaks in tongues is strengthened personally,"*

The word *"edify"* in the Greek literally means *"to charge, like charging a battery,"* like when your cell phone dies and you've got to plug it into a power source to charge the battery. When you speak in tongues, you are plugging your spirit into a power source—the Holy Spirit—to charge your spirit!

The word *"edify"* also means *"to build, as in building a house; to rebuild; to repair; to strengthen."*

Proverbs 18:14 says:

> *"¹⁴ A man's spirit sustains him in sickness, but a crushed spirit who can bear?"*

The Amplified Bible (AMPC) says:

> *"¹⁴ The strong spirit of a man sustains him in bodily pain or trouble, but a weak and broken spirit who can raise up or bear?"*

One of the definitions of the word *"sustain"* in the Hebrew text (the Old Testament was written mostly in Hebrew) is *"to sustain, support, nourish."* When you're sick or having any problems, speaking in tongues will strengthen your spirit which in turn will sustain, support, and nourish you during sickness and difficult times. It will help you greatly to remain strong in those situations and get through those times of hardship more quickly.

Reading and meditating on the Word of God will also strengthen your spirit because the Word of God is food for your spirit (Matthew 4:4; Hebrews 5:12; 1 Peter 2:2).

So speaking in tongues charges your spirit, builds you up, and strengthens your inner man with might to carry you through life! Praise God for this gift! When you need a charge, speak in tongues!

## #6 Speaking in Tongues Gives Spiritual Refreshing

Similarly, speaking in tongues gives spiritual refreshing. Isaiah 28:11–12 (KJV) say:

> *"¹¹ For with stammering lips and another tongue will he speak to this people. ¹² To whom he said, This is the **rest** wherewith ye may cause the weary to **rest**; and this is the **refreshing**: yet they would not hear."*

Regarding speaking with stammering lips and another tongue, Isaiah says, *"This is the rest* for the weary, and *this is the refreshing."* So there is refreshing and a rest for your spirit when you speak in tongues.

When you need refreshing, speak in tongues! You can take this rest cure every day!

## #7 Speaking in Tongues Stirs Up the Well & Causes the River to Flow Within You

When you get born again, your spirit is made new and is filled with the *zoe* life of God (eternal life). That *life* becomes a well inside of you—in your spirit—a well springing up to eternal life, the *zoe* God-kind of life. John 4:10,14 say:

> *"10 Jesus answered her, 'If you knew the gift of God and who it is that asks you for a drink, you would have asked him and he would have given you **living water**.' 14 but whoever drinks the water I give him will never thirst. Indeed, **the water I give him will become in him a spring of water welling up to eternal life.**'"*

Sometimes wells can be capped, but speaking in tongues uncaps the well. It stirs up that well in your spirit and causes it to overflow into a river! As Jesus said in John 7:38–39:

> *"38 'Whoever believes in me, as the Scripture has said, **streams of living water will flow from within him.'** 39 **By this he meant the Spirit**, whom those who believed in him were later to receive. Up to that time the Spirit had not been given, since Jesus had not yet been glorified."*

Speaking in tongues causes the river of the Holy Spirit to flow in you. Many people have this testimony that when they speak in tongues, it feels like a river is coming out from their spirit through their mouth. Speaking in tongues makes you feel like you're in a river and it's flowing out from within you!

When you have this river flowing in you, your spirit is like a well-watered garden. Isaiah 58:11 says:

> *"11 The LORD will guide you always; he will satisfy your needs in a sun-scorched land and will strengthen your frame.* **You will be like a well-watered garden, like a spring whose waters never fail.***"*

This happens when you speak in tongues frequently and regularly. It keeps your spirit well-watered!

## #8 Speaking in Tongues Is Drinking in the Spirit

And then at the same time, speaking in tongues is also taking a drink of those rivers of the Holy Spirit flowing in you. When you're speaking in tongues, you are actually drinking of the Holy Spirit, because the water of life is flowing in you, and you're drinking it while you're speaking.

Again, John 4:10–14 say:

> *"10 Jesus answered her, 'If you knew the gift of God and who it is that asks you for a drink, you would*

> have asked him and he would have given you living water.' [11] 'Sir,' the woman said, 'you have nothing to draw with and the well is deep. Where can you get this living water? [12] Are you greater than our father Jacob, who gave us the well and drank from it himself, as did also his sons and his flocks and herds?' [13] Jesus answered, 'Everyone who drinks this water will be thirsty again, [14] but whoever **drinks the water I give him** will never thirst. Indeed, the water I give him will become in him a spring of water welling up to eternal life.'"

And again, John 7:37–39 say:

> "[37] On the last and greatest day of the Feast, Jesus stood and said in a loud voice, 'If anyone is thirsty, let him come to me and **drink**. [38] Whoever believes in me, as the Scripture has said, streams of living water will flow from within him.' [39] By this he meant the Spirit, whom those who believed in him were later to receive. Up to that time the Spirit had not been given, since Jesus had not yet been glorified."

Jesus said that we could *"drink"* from the streams of living water flowing from within us by the Holy Spirit. The New Testament Greek word translated *"drink"* means *"to quaff; to imbibe; to get drunk."* *"Quaff"* means *"to drink down in big gulps."*

In Acts 2:4–18, we read:

*"⁴ All of them were **filled with the Holy Spirit and began to speak in other tongues** as the Spirit enabled them. ⁵ Now there were staying in Jerusalem God-fearing Jews from every nation under heaven. ⁶ When they heard this sound, a crowd came together in bewilderment, because each one heard them speaking in his own language. ⁷ Utterly amazed, they asked: 'Are not all these men who are speaking Galileans? ⁸ Then how is it that each of us hears them in his own native language? ⁹ Parthians, Medes and Elamites; residents of Mesopotamia, Judea and Cappadocia, Pontus and Asia, ¹⁰ Phrygia and Pamphylia, Egypt and the parts of Libya near Cyrene; visitors from Rome ¹¹ (both Jews and converts to Judaism); Cretans and Arabs—we hear them declaring the wonders of God in our own tongues!' ¹² Amazed and perplexed, they asked one another, 'What does this mean?' ¹³ Some, however, made fun of them and said, **'They have had too much wine.'** ¹⁴ Then Peter stood up with the Eleven, raised his voice and addressed the crowd: 'Fellow Jews and all of you who live in Jerusalem, let me explain this to you; listen carefully to what I say. ¹⁵ **These men are not drunk, as you suppose.** It's only nine in the morning! ¹⁶ No, this is what was spoken by the prophet Joel: ¹⁷ 'In the last days, God says, **I will pour out my Spirit on all people.** Your sons and daughters will prophesy, your young men will see visions, your old men will dream dreams. ¹⁸ Even on my servants, both men and women, I will pour out my Spirit in those days, and they will prophesy."*

Notice that when the disciples began speaking in tongues, other people thought they were drunk! Sometimes when you speak in tongues, especially under a very strong anointing, it even feels like you get "high." It is because the Holy Spirit has come upon you!

Ephesians 5:18 says:

*"18 Do not get drunk on wine, which leads to debauchery.* **Instead, be filled with the Spirit.***"*

Notice here that the scripture is comparing being filled with the Holy Spirit to being drunk on wine! You can literally get drunk in the Spirit! But that usually only happens when you are under a very strong anointing or when you speak in tongues for a long time. Usually when you speak in tongues, you are just drinking but not getting drunk. However, you *are* satisfying a spiritual thirst. Thank God for this gift!

## #9 Speaking in Tongues Makes Us God-Inside Conscious

Another reason for speaking in tongues is that it makes us conscious of God's presence inside of us. It makes us aware of the Holy Spirit in us. It reminds us of the indwelling presence of the Holy Spirit. John 14:16–17 say:

> *"¹⁶ And I will ask the Father, and he will give you another Counselor to be with you forever— ¹⁷ the Spirit of truth. The world cannot accept him, because it neither sees him nor knows him. But you know him, for he lives with you and **will be in you**."*

Many Christians say they don't "feel" God's presence. Many Christians live their daily lives without an awareness of God's presence. Speaking in tongues makes you very much God-inside minded! You are very aware "God is in me" because He is flowing and moving in you, and you are speaking by the unction and inspiration of the Holy Spirit!

## #10 Speaking in Tongues Develops Intimacy With the Holy Spirit

Speaking in tongues also develops intimacy with the Holy Spirit because it is your private conversation with God. It's a spirit-to-Spirit communication. When you speak in tongues, you are fellowshipping with the Holy Spirit intimately.

Tongues, I believe, is also what Psalm 42:7 is talking about:

> *"⁷ Deep calls to deep in the roar of your waterfalls; all your waves and breakers have swept over me."*

I think of the waterfalls, waves, and breakers in this verse as the Holy Spirit coming upon us and moving in and through us. Remember, Jesus compared the Holy Spirit in us to a river.

Here, the Psalmist talks about *"deep calling unto deep in the roar of your waterfalls."* What is that? It's the "deep" inside of you calling to the "deep" inside of God! It's your spirit connecting with God's Spirit in a very intimate way.

Romans 8:26 says:

> *"26 In the same way, the Spirit helps us in our weakness. We do not know what we ought to pray for, but the Spirit himself intercedes for us with groans that words cannot express."*

This "groaning" includes tongues. You can groan, you can cry, and you can say things in tongues from the very depth of your being—things that you could never put into English (or your own language). Sometimes there are things you cannot express with your understanding, and so the Holy Spirit helps you.

When you feel like saying, "God, you know my heart about this, but I just don't know how to say it," let the deep in you call to the deep in God! Let the Holy Spirit in you express it in tongues!

## #11 Speaking in Tongues Increases Your Sensitivity to the Holy Spirit

Speaking in tongues tunes you in to the Holy Spirit and increases your sensitivity to the Holy Spirit, helping you to be more led by the Holy Spirit. It's like tuning in the old-fashioned radios, especially to a faint station. You've got to work to tune it until you get right on the station to eliminate static and get a clear signal. Sometimes when we want to hear from God, we are getting too much static from our flesh, other people, and the world around us. When you speak in tongues, you are fine-tuning your spirit into the "frequency" of the Holy Spirit and sensitizing your spirit to the voice of God!

## #12 Speaking in Tongues Helps You Control Your Flesh & Overcome Sin

If you are continually aware of the presence of the Holy Spirit in you, it will help you bring your flesh under subjection and resist sin and temptation. It helps you live more godly and more spiritually. Why? Because you're not going to sin right in front of the Holy Spirit!

If you're consciously aware "God is in me" by speaking in tongues, you're not going to go out and get drunk. You're not going to curse and speak foul language. You're not going to commit adultery. It will even help you control your temper. That constant awareness of God's presence in you and that connection with God helps to set you apart and sanctify you from the sinfulness in the world and fleshiness or carnality. It empowers you!

As I already said, the baptism in the Holy Spirit and speaking in tongues bring the power of God into our lives because the Holy Spirit *is* the power of God. It is being endued (clothed) with power from on high. As Jesus said in Luke 24:49:

> *"49 I am going to send you what my Father has promised; but stay in the city until you have been* **clothed** [KJV – *endued*] **with power from on high."'**

Acts 1:8 says:

> *"8 But you will* **receive power** *when the Holy Spirit comes* **on** *you…"*

There is a clothing of power when you receive the baptism in the Holy Spirit! And when you speak in tongues, it stirs up and increases that power within you (as I said earlier, it charges your spirit!). This power also helps you overcome temptation and live godly.

As the grace of God *teaches* us, the Holy Spirit *empowers* us:

> *"…to say 'No' to ungodliness and worldly passions, and to live self-controlled, upright and godly lives in this present age"* (Titus 2:12).

His presence helps you control your flesh. It's *"by the Spirit"* that we resist and overcome sin. Galatians 5:16 says:

*"16 So I say, **live by the Spirit**, and you will not gratify the desires of the sinful nature."*

Romans 8:5–7,9,13 say:

*"5 Those who live according to the sinful nature have their minds set on what that nature desires; but those who **live in accordance with the Spirit have their minds set on what the Spirit desires**. 6 The mind of sinful man is death, but **the mind controlled by the Spirit is life and peace**; 7 the sinful mind is hostile to God. It does not submit to God's law, nor can it do so. 9 **You, however, are controlled not by the sinful nature but by the Spirit, if the Spirit of God lives in you**. And if anyone does not have the Spirit of Christ, he does not belong to Christ. 13 ...if **by the Spirit you put to death the misdeeds of the body**, you will live."*

Speaking in tongues also helps you control your tongue. When you speak in tongues, you have to yield your tongue to say what God wants you to say. As I said before, the Holy Spirit teaches you what to say, but you have to say it as an act of your will and an act of obedience by faith. That is when you are yielding your tongue to God.

James 3:8 says:

> *"8 but no man can tame the tongue. It is a restless evil, full of deadly poison."*

Yes, no *man* can tame the tongue, but the Holy Spirit can! When you speak in tongues, you are taming your tongue. You're getting that "wild lion" tongue tamed under the control of the Holy Spirit, and it will help you then to control your tongue at other times as well.

So when you're tempted to sin, or say or do something you shouldn't, start speaking in tongues. It helps your spirit rise up to dominate your flesh with the power of the Holy Spirit!

## #13 Speaking in Tongues Is a Way of Keeping Free From Worldly Contamination

Speaking in tongues is also a way of keeping free from worldly contamination around you. When you see and hear unclean things in the world, it makes you unclean. It doesn't make your spirit unclean, because nothing can touch that. But it makes your eyes, ears, and mind unclean. For example, when you go into a public restroom and there are dirty words on the walls, or when people are saying things around you—cussing or telling dirty jokes or gossip—that you don't want to hear, it makes your eyes, ears, and mind unclean. You will probably even feel defiled. That's when you need to wash yourself in the blood of Jesus (listen to my teaching on *"The Power of the Blood of Jesus"* on YouTube). But if you will speak in tongues when you see and hear those things, it will keep those things from defiling you.

Again, John 4:14 says:

*"¹⁴ but whoever drinks the water I give him will never thirst. Indeed, the water I give him will become in him a **spring of water welling up** to eternal life.'"*

As we read in John 7:37–39:

*"³⁷ On the last and greatest day of the Feast, Jesus stood and said in a loud voice, 'If anyone is thirsty, let him come to me and drink. ³⁸ Whoever believes in me, as the Scripture has said, **streams of living water will flow from within him.'** ³⁹ By this he meant the Spirit, whom those who believed in him were later to receive. Up to that time the Spirit had not been given, since Jesus had not yet been glorified."*

We have all seen water fountains. Consider a big water fountain with water shooting upward with great force. If you wad up a piece of paper into a ball and throw it into the fountain while the water is shooting upward, what happens to the wad of paper? It gets shot out of the fountain by the force of the water. Nothing can get in when there's a flow coming out! The force of shooting water doesn't allow anything to get into the hole that the water flows from. Likewise, when you speak in tongues, you're keeping that inner well springing up and the river flowing in you. When you do that, you're keeping garbage out because that well springing up from your spirit is like a fountain bubbling up when you speak in tongues!

So when you see or hear things around you that are unclean—no matter where you are—you can start speaking in tongues quietly under your breath. By doing so, you're getting that fountain of *zoe* life to spring up and shoot out of your spirit with the force of eternal life which will stop all of that garbage from getting in and defiling you. So, speaking in tongues keeps you free from worldly contamination. Praise God!

## #14 Praying in Tongues Enables Us to Pray for the Unknown

Praying in tongues enables us to pray for the unknown. First Corinthians 14:14–15 say:

> *"14 For if I pray in a tongue, my spirit prays, but my mind [KJV – understanding] is unfruitful. 15 So what shall I do? I will pray with my spirit, but I will also pray with my mind [KJV – understanding]; I will sing with my spirit, but I will also sing with my mind [KJV – understanding]."*

Notice verse 15 says, *"I will pray with my spirit, but I will also pray with my mind."* As was mentioned earlier regarding singing with your spirit and with understanding, that means praying with your spirit is *not* praying with your mind. Paul is differentiating between praying *with* understanding and praying *without* understanding. You can only pray without understanding when you pray in tongues.

In verse 14, Paul said, *"if I pray in a tongue, my spirit prays* [as taught and inspired by the Holy Spirit], *but my mind* [KJV – *understanding*] *is unfruitful."*

You can have *anointed, inspired-by-the-Holy-Spirit* prayer in your known language, with your understanding, but it's different when you pray in tongues. Then, you're not using your mind. It's flowing directly from your spirit by the Holy Spirit out of your mouth in an unknown language, and your mind is *"unfruitful."* **Since the Holy Spirit is praying through you, and yet you don't have understanding of what you're praying,** *you are praying unknown things to you by the inspiration of the Holy Spirit! You're speaking mysteries!*

## #15 Speaking in Tongues Gives Us Access to Understand the Mysteries of God

Look at 1 Corinthians 14:2:

*"2 For anyone who speaks in a tongue does not speak to men but to God. Indeed, no one understands him; he utters **mysteries** with his spirit."*

67

Then also 1 Corinthians 2:7:

*"7 No, we speak of God's **secret wisdom**, a wisdom that has been **hidden** and that God destined for our glory before time began."*

The New King James Version (NKJV) says:

*"7 But we speak the wisdom of God in a **mystery**, the **hidden** wisdom which God ordained before the ages for our glory,"*

The word *"mystery"* in these verses is the Greek word *"musterion,"* which means *"hidden thing, secret, mystery, coded secret."* God has coded secrets!

The word *"hidden"* means *"to hide, to keep secret."*

Then continuing with 1 Corinthians 2:8–13:

*"8 **None of the rulers of this age understood it**, for if they had, they would not have crucified the Lord of glory. 9 However, as it is written: 'No eye has seen, no ear has heard, no mind has conceived what God has prepared for those who love him'— 10 but **God has revealed it to us by his Spirit**. The Spirit searches all things, even the deep things of God. 11 For who among men knows the thoughts of a man except the man's spirit within him? In the same way, no one knows **the thoughts of God** except the Spirit of God. 12 We have not received the spirit of the*

> *world but the Spirit who is from God, **that we may understand** what God has freely given us.*
> *13 **This is what we speak, not in words taught us by human wisdom but in words taught by the Spirit, expressing spiritual truths in spiritual words.***"

Speaking in tongues is speaking *"the thoughts of God"* (verse 11) — God's knowledge, counsel, wisdom, mysteries, and coded secrets which are hidden from the wicked (verses 7 and 8). You don't know what they are, but when you pray in tongues, you're praying out God's coded secrets! Wow! Praise God! So ***praying in tongues is drawing and receiving the secrets of God into your life's complicated issues***. When you receive the interpretation (we'll talk more about that later), you are getting revelation of those things that are concealed or hidden. Hallelujah!

God has answers for all your questions and situations, and He has solutions for all your problems. When you pray in tongues, you are praying God's secret wisdom—you are praying out the answers, solutions, guidance, and direction that you need! This is a powerful way to get the *supernatural help* from God that you need. When you need answers and guidance, pray in tongues!

## #16 Speaking in Tongues Gives Us Access to the "Spirit of Wisdom and Revelation"

Speaking in tongues gives us access to the *"Spirit of wisdom and revelation in the knowledge of him."*

Look at Ephesians 1:17 in the King James Version (KJV):

> *"17 That the God of our Lord Jesus Christ, the Father of glory, may give unto you* **the spirit of wisdom and revelation in the knowledge of him:"**

Ephesians 1:17–19 (NIV) say:

> *"17 I keep asking that the God of our Lord Jesus Christ, the glorious Father, may give you* **the Spirit of wisdom and revelation, so that you may know him better.** *18 I pray also that* **the eyes of your heart may be enlightened in order that you may know** *the hope to which he has called you, the riches of his glorious inheritance in the saints,* *19 and his incomparably great power for us who believe."*

I have discovered and witnessed again and again that people who do not speak in tongues (even Christians who have been baptized in the Holy Spirit at one time but do not speak in tongues regularly), do not seem to have *"the Spirit of wisdom and revelation in the knowledge of him."* The eyes of their heart are not "enlightened," and they have a hard time understanding the scriptures and do not seem to be able to understand God, His Word, and His ways. (I can tell the difference in the understanding of what I am saying when I am speaking to people who have been baptized in the Holy Spirit and when I am speaking to people who have not been baptized in the Holy Spirit.) Many Christians who have been baptized in the Holy Spirit and speak in tongues *regularly* (that is a key), can testify that their spiritual knowledge and understanding of God and His Word greatly increased *after* they were baptized in the Holy Spirit. They began getting "revelation" and understanding of the Word of God. Why? Because this revelation comes through the Holy Spirit when you speak in tongues.

## #17 When We Pray in Tongues, the Holy Spirit Is Interceding for Us

When we pray in tongues, the Holy Spirit is interceding for us. Romans 8:26–27 say:

> *"26 In the same way, the Spirit helps us in our weakness. We do not know what we ought to pray for, but **the Spirit himself intercedes for us** with groans that words cannot express. 27 And he who searches our hearts knows the mind of the Spirit, because **the Spirit intercedes for the saints** in accordance with God's will."*

Praise God! We have an intercessor besides ourselves! When we pray in tongues, the Holy Spirit is interceding for us!

## #18 Praying in Tongues Is Praying God's Perfect Will

Another reason to pray in tongues is because it is praying God's perfect will. Romans 8:26–27 say:

*"26 In the same way, the Spirit helps us in our weakness. We do not know what we ought to pray for, but the Spirit himself intercedes for us with groans that words cannot express. 27 And he who searches our hearts knows the mind of the Spirit, because the Spirit intercedes for the saints* **in accordance with God's will.***"*

Someone who was against speaking in tongues said to me one time, "Well, I know what I ought to pray for." That's just pride. You think you know, but there's a lot you don't know, and a lot of what you're saying could be wrong. This scripture says, *"We do not know what we ought to pray for."* That's the truth. But the Holy Spirit was sent to help us pray, and He intercedes for us with *"groans that words cannot express."* This also includes tongues.

When you pray in tongues, there is no way you can pray wrong. There is no way you can pray selfish, greedy, prideful, or manipulative prayers (praying your own ideas or your own will regarding the subject of prayer) because God is praying through you. You don't know what you're saying, so *you are not influencing your prayers with sinful, carnal desires or attitudes.*

In our own language, we can even pray for the wrong thing. We're saying, "Oh God, give me this one, give me this one," but God says, "No, that's not the right one for you. This is the right one for you." Or we might be praying, "Oh God, please do this," but He is saying, "No, that's not what should be done. This is what needs to be done." Because of our lack of knowledge of so many things, you can be praying for the wrong thing and not know it.

But when you're praying in tongues, you'll always be praying the right thing the right way. You'll always be praying the perfect will of God. There will be no error in it. There will be no pride, greed, selfishness, or wrong motive in it. It will always be perfect because it's the Spirit of God praying. Praise God!

# #19 Speaking in Tongues Is Praying, Prophesying, & Decreeing God's Plan For Your Future

Speaking in tongues is also prophesying and praying out God's plan for your future. You could be praying about what you will be doing next year or five years from now, and God is working now ahead of time to bring it to pass.

Speaking in tongues is decreeing the plan of God. We need to make faith declarations and decrees of the Word of God on a continual basis, which we can do simply by taking scriptures and speaking them. However, speaking in tongues is also decreeing the will of God over your life or other people and situations to establish it and bring it to pass. They are life-filled, faith-filled, and anointing-filled words being spoken over the person or situation the Holy Spirit is praying for through you.

Tongues can also release the angels to work and minister in a situation because some of the languages are the languages of angels. I believe many times it activates our angels on heavenly assignments— assignments God is giving them to do for us. When you pray in tongues, you could be commissioning and sending your angels when you don't even know it. God is doing it for you!

## #20 Praying in Tongues Uses "Most Holy Faith"

Mark 11:24 says:

*"24 Therefore I tell you, whatever you ask for in prayer, **believe that you have received it**, and it will be yours."*

When we pray, we must *believe* that we *have* received what we asked for. That is what we call exercising or using our faith when we pray. But if we have doubt or fear mixed with our faith, it defiles or contaminates our faith. I've heard it said, "Fear tolerated is faith contaminated." Faith mixed with fear or doubt is not pure faith and therefore is not as effective as pure faith—it does not always bring the results we want.

Jude 1:20 (NKJV) says:

*"20 But you, beloved, building yourselves up on your* **most holy faith, praying in the Holy Spirit,***"*

What is "most holy faith"? It's perfect, pure faith—faith that is undefiled and uncontaminated with fear and doubt. When you pray with your understanding, you can always be tempted to doubt that you receive what you have asked for.

When you pray in tongues, you are probably always praying for things that are bigger and greater than your faith can believe to receive because God is so much bigger than us and His plans are so much bigger! If you knew what you were praying in tongues, it would probably give your faith a heart attack! But because you don't know what you said, you cannot think, "Oh, God, how can I ever do that? How can I ever have that? It's too big for me, it's too much," or "How could that ever happen?" You cannot doubt it, you cannot be in unbelief, you cannot have fear, and you cannot be intimidated by it. Therefore, it's perfect faith! It's uncontaminated by your own thoughts and doubts!

Also, when you pray in tongues, as we said already, you know you are praying the perfect will of God, so you can be confident and have faith to receive it. So, *after you finish praying in tongues you should say, "Lord, I believe I receive everything I just prayed in tongues."* By doing that, you are *activating and releasing your faith* to receive what you said in tongues.

## #22 Speaking in Tongues Gives Physical Health Benefits

The last benefits I want to mention are actual physical and emotional health benefits that come to people who pray in tongues. This is based on medical and scientific research studies.

Dr. Carl Peterson, M.D. did research[3] on the relationship between the brain and speaking in tongues. He discovered that "As we engage in our heavenly language, the brain releases two chemical secretions that are directed into our immune system giving a 35 to 40 percent boost to the immune system. This promotes healing within our bodies. Amazingly, this secretion is triggered from a part of the brain that has no other apparent activity in humans and is only activated by our Spirit-led prayer and worship…. As we exercise our life in the Spirit by speaking in our heavenly language that He has put within us, we are touching the supernatural power of God, and we are letting Him restore part of what was lost."

Hallelujah! There is an immune system boost when you pray in tongues.

## #23 Speaking in Tongues Calms Your Attitude & Your Mood

Another study[4] shows speaking in tongues "is associated with a reduction in stress in response to normal stressors and significantly associated with positive mood and calmness." Obviously, the reduction of stress is extremely helpful to one's immune system and entire health because stress damages the body. Peace heals the body.

In the tests they did on people while they were speaking in tongues, there was what the Bible calls "peace that passes understanding." They were able to medically document the reduction of stress and the positive mood and calmness of those speaking in tongues.

Another study[5] of nearly 1,000 Christians found that those who engaged in the practice of speaking tongues were more emotionally stable than those who did not speak in tongues.

Then in another study[6], "researchers at the University of Pennsylvania took brain images of five women while they spoke in tongues and found that their frontal lobes—the thinking, willful part of the brain through which people control what they do—were relatively quiet, as were the language centers. The regions involved in maintaining self-consciousness [alertness] were active [in other words, the women were not in blind trances]. The new findings contrasted sharply with images taken of other spiritually inspired mental states like meditation, which is often a highly focused mental exercise, activating the frontal lobes." So whereas meditation activates the frontal lobes, speaking in tongues quiets the frontal lobes.

I heard a preacher referring to this one time, and he said, "I'm going to deactivate my frontal lobes for a while," meaning he was going to pray in tongues for a while! That sounds kind of funny, but that's actually what you're doing when you're quietly setting yourself aside to speak in tongues and not engaging in anything else. (Of course, doing other active things while praying in tongues keeps the frontal lobes active.)

## Interpreting Your Tongues

First Corinthians 14:13 says:

> *"13 For this reason anyone who speaks in a tongue should pray that he may interpret what he says."*

This shows us that we can pray for the interpretation of our tongues because there are things that God wants us to know and understand, as we already read in 1 Corinthians 2:7–13:

> *"⁷ No, we speak of God's **secret wisdom**, a wisdom that has been **hidden** and that God destined for our glory before time began. ⁸ None of the rulers of this age understood it, for if they had, they would not have crucified the Lord of glory. ⁹ However, as it is written: 'No eye has seen, no ear has heard, no mind has conceived what God has prepared for those who love him'—¹⁰ but **God has revealed it to us by his Spirit**. The Spirit searches all things, even the deep things of God. ¹¹ For who among men knows the thoughts of a man except the man's spirit within him? In the same way no one knows the thoughts of God except the Spirit of God. ¹² We have not received the spirit of the world but the Spirit who is from God, **that we may understand what God has freely given us. ¹³ This is what we speak, not in words taught us by human wisdom but in words taught by the Spirit, expressing spiritual truths in spiritual words.***"

In private or personal tongues, most of the time, you will not get a word-for-word interpretation or know exactly what you're saying in tongues, but you can often get a sense of the general subject you're praying about by what's in your heart. You can tell when you're praising and worshiping the Lord because it's in the spirit of praise, and praise is in your heart.

You can tell when you're interceding because the spirit of intercession comes on you and there's a moving in your spirit to pray for something or someone, or you will get something or someone on your mind that you have a burden to pray for. It might be a situation, your spouse, your children, your friend, your finances, your country, or even another country, and you know you're interceding for them or that situation because it's in your heart, and it's coming out of your spirit in tongues. You might have your job on your heart, and you're thinking, "Oh, my job, God help me on my job, babababababa (tongues)." Then you know you're praying about your job because that's what's in your heart when you're praying.

However, much of the time when you're speaking in tongues throughout the day, you will not even get a sense of what you are talking about. God knows, and that's all that matters because you are communicating to Him. If He wants you to know, He'll tell you. But oftentimes, He knows that if He tells you, you'll mess it up or you wouldn't believe it—you'd be in doubt and unbelief about what He is inspiring you to say, or if it's about someone else, it's none of your business. He just needs you to pray. So He reveals it to you only on a need-to-know basis.

You can also choose what or who to pray for and begin by saying, "Lord, I pray for such-and-such," and then start speaking in tongues. You can know that God will pray through you for the thing you have asked about.

You can ask God for wisdom, answers, solutions, and direction you need in your life to be revealed to you, and then sometimes you get an idea immediately while you're praying in tongues, but often the interpretation of your tongues comes hours, days, or weeks later in the form of God-ideas, insights, revelations, and leadings and promptings from the Holy Spirit because when you speak in tongues you are "downloading" the mysteries and wisdom into your spirit, like downloading something from the internet. In those cases, I find that I don't get an immediate word-for-word interpretation of my tongues while I'm praying, such as, "Cherri, thou shalt go to India." It usually comes in the days and weeks that follow as enlightenment, understanding, revelation, ideas—even divine connections, and I get the direction I'm looking for. For example, you might have asked for a solution for something and then started praying in tongues. Then a few days later you get an idea and you think, *"I know how to fix that. I know what to do about that." That was the answer you had prayed for in tongues.*

However, it also comes on a need-to-know basis, so if you are in a situation that you need immediate guidance for, and you are asking the Lord, "What should I do?" then as you pray in tongues, you can get the answer or leading that you need. This is part of practicing following the leading of the Holy Spirit (listen to my radio broadcast series on YouTube called *"How to Be Led by the Holy Spirit"* to learn more).

# Chapter Four

# How To Receive the Baptism in the Holy Spirit

L ast of all, how do you receive the baptism in the Holy Spirit? It's so simple! Like I said, I think I have helped people receive the baptism in the Holy Spirit with speaking in tongues in almost every country I've been to because it's really very easy and very simple.

## #1 The Holy Spirit Is Ready!

First, realize the Holy Spirit is ready and waiting for *you* to receive. You are not waiting for Him to decide to baptize you. He came on the Day of Pentecost in Acts 2 and has never left. He's here *now* for you to receive the baptism in the Holy Spirit. You can receive Him right now!

## #2 You Will Not Receive a Counterfeit

Second, don't be concerned that it won't be the Holy Spirit speaking through you (this is a common concern). You must have faith and trust God. Luke 11:11–13 say:

> *"11 Which of you fathers, if your son asks for a fish, will give him a snake instead? 12 Or if he asks for an egg, will give him a scorpion? 13 If you then, though you are evil, know how to give good gifts to your children, how much more will your Father in heaven give the Holy Spirit to those who ask him!"'*

You're not going to give your son a snake when he asks for a fish. In the same way, you will not receive a counterfeit. You will get exactly what you ask for. God will give you the baptism in the Holy Spirit when you ask for it!

## #3 You Must Be Born Again

Third, the only prerequisite is that you must be born again[1]. Your first experience with the Holy Spirit is receiving Him *in* you in the new birth. The second experience is to receive the Holy Spirit *upon* you in the baptism in the Holy Spirit. So, if you've not been born again, if you don't have Jesus in you, take care of that first. Simply say, "Lord Jesus, come into my heart. I ask you to be my Lord and Savior. I give you my life right now, in Jesus' Name, Amen." Now you're born again! Praise God!

## #4 Ask!

Fourth, you must *ask* God for the baptism in the Holy Spirit. James 4:2 says:

*"2 You do not have, because you do not ask God."*

Luke 11:9–10 say:

*"9 'So I say to you: Ask and it will be given to you; seek and you will find; knock and the door will be opened to you. 10 For everyone who asks receives; he who seeks finds; and to him who knocks, the door will be opened.'"*

And again, Luke 11:13 says:

*"13 'If you then, though you are evil, know how to give good gifts to your children, how much more will your Father in heaven give the Holy Spirit to those who **ask** him!'"*

So simply *ask* the Father for the baptism in the Holy Spirit with speaking in tongues, and He will give it to you *immediately*! Just say, *"Father, I ask you for the baptism in the Holy Spirit and for the gift of speaking in tongues. I ask you to baptize me right now, in Jesus' Name."*

## #5 Believe You Receive

Then, number five is the principle of faith. Mark 11:24 says:

*"24 Therefore I tell you, whatever you ask for in prayer, believe that you have received it, and it will be yours."*

When you ask, you must believe you receive it **immediately**. Say, *"Thank you, Father, I believe I receive it."*

## #6 Start Speaking in Tongues

The last thing is, if you believe you receive, then *you* just start speaking in tongues following the promptings of the Holy Spirit inside of you. You switch from your known language into tongues *by faith*.

As I gave you the example already, let me show you again. Say, "käpingä köht." If you just said that, you did it because you copied me. I *taught* you what to say, and you trusted me and willingly chose to say it. It's the same with receiving the baptism in the Holy Spirit and the gift of speaking in tongues. The Holy Spirit prompts you *what* to say, but He doesn't make you say it. You start following those promptings, speaking them out loud. **Start saying any sounds or syllables that come to you other than your known**

**language.** It *will* sound weird! Especially at first when you are unfamiliar with it. It might sound like baby gibberish or it might sound like stuttering, but you just start saying it. Don't hold back or be timid. **Be bold to speak it out loud.** Once you begin, it will start flowing, and the more you practice, the more it will flow—first a trickle, then a stream, then a river, then a flood will flow through your lips from your spirit! Praise God!

Remember, you're seeking God and you're seeking the Holy Spirit. You're not just seeking tongues as a gift of God, but you're seeking a greater measure of God in your life. When you ask and seek, you will receive! Praise the Lord!

So *ask, believe you receive* **when you ask**, *and then just start doing it.* Open your mouth and start speaking out loud by faith whatever promptings and inspiration you get. That's how easy it is! God is ready. Are you?

## Like A Child

The very few occasions where I've met someone who wants to speak in tongues but has not been able to have been with people who are highly intelligent intellectuals. It seems that they have a hard time starting to speak what seems like to them as gibberish. But remember what Jesus said in Matthew 18:3:

> *"³ And he said: 'I tell you the truth, unless you change and become like little children, you will never enter the kingdom of heaven.'"*

As it is with being born again, it is the same with receiving the baptism in the Holy Spirit with the gift of speaking in tongues—you must become like a little child!

Jesus also said in Matthew 11:25:

> *"²⁵ ... I praise you, Father, Lord of heaven and earth, because you have hidden these things from the wise and learned, and revealed them to little children.'"*

And Paul wrote in 1 Corinthians 1:27:

> *"²⁷ But God chose the foolish things of the world to shame the wise;"*

This reveals another reason why some people do not speak in tongues—because of pride. They are too proud to speak words that sound like gibberish. So a person has to humble himself and become like a little child to speak in tongues. But isn't that the same way a person gets saved? They have to humble themselves before God and become like a little child. It is the same with speaking in tongues.

# Speaking In Tongues Is A
# Spiritual Discipline

Just like reading your Bible and praying are spiritual disciplines that you have to develop and make a habit of practicing every day, so is speaking in tongues. You will usually have to make a conscious effort to begin speaking in tongues because your mind is always busy with all the daily activities of life. And just like reading your Bible and praying in your known language help you to grow and be strengthened spiritually, so does speaking in tongues. It is a spiritual discipline that is *very* beneficial, as I've already shared about the many spiritual, mental, and physical benefits of speaking in tongues.

## Speak in Tongues Anytime, Anywhere!

As I said earlier, Paul said in 1 Corinthians 14:18:

*"18 I thank God that I speak in tongues more than all of you."*

How could he speak in tongues more than all of those in the church in Corinth? He must have spoken in tongues all the time! (This shows the importance of speaking in tongues.)

You can speak in tongues anytime, anywhere. You don't have to be in your prayer closet, and you don't have to be in church. You can speak in tongues at home, at work, in the store, while you walk down the street, and while driving on the road (that's a good place to speak in tongues!). You can speak in tongues while you take a shower, while you're washing dishes, working, or washing your car. You can speak in tongues while you do anything!

## The Holy Spirit Is Always On

Somebody asked one time, "But how can you turn the Holy Spirit on and off?" You don't. *The Holy Spirit is always on.* He's always there. God is always on. He's never off. The Spirit is always on. He's never off. It's a matter of you tuning in your spirit "radio" to Him. Just like in the natural, there are always radio signals in the atmosphere. To hear those signals, you must turn on a radio and tune in to a station. You tune in to that frequency. In the same way, the Holy Spirit is always on but you tune *yourself* in. You turn *yourself* on and off. You are in control of yourself. You can start talking in tongues and stop talking in tongues at your own will, just like you can start and stop talking in your known language at your own will. So you can do it anytime, anywhere. **Just do it!**

Speaking, praying, and praising God in tongues is a powerful tool and weapon for your everyday life. I encourage you to make use of this precious gift from God every single day! The more you do it, the more you will see it greatly enrich your life!

# Notes

1 Born again: John 3:3–6 (NKJV) say:

> *"3 Jesus answered and said to him, 'Most assuredly, I say to you, unless one is born again, he cannot see the kingdom of God.' 4 Nicodemus said to Him, 'How can a man be born when he is old? Can he enter a second time into his mother's womb and be born?' 5 Jesus answered, 'Most assuredly, I say to you, unless one is born of water and the Spirit, he cannot enter the kingdom of God. 6 That which is born of the flesh is flesh, and that which is born of the Spirit is spirit.'"*

Also, 1 Peter 1:21,23 say:

> *"21 **Through him you believe in God, who raised him from the dead and glorified him**, and so your **faith and hope are in God**. 23 For you have been **born again**, not of perishable seed, but of imperishable, through the living and enduring word of God."*

Being born again means your spirit is made new by the power of God. Second Corinthians 5:17 says you are a new creation on the inside:

> *"17 Therefore, if anyone is in Christ, he is a new creation; the old has gone, the new has come!"*

91

When you believe in and receive Jesus Christ as your personal Savior, you are born into God's family becoming one of His children, as it says in John 1:12–13:

> "*12 Yet to all who received him, to those who* **believed in his name**, *he gave the right to* **become children of God**— *13 children born not of natural descent, nor of human decision or a husband's will, but* **born of God**."

## How To Be Born Again

Acts 16:30–31 say:

> "*30 He then brought them out and asked, 'Sirs, what must I do to be saved?' 31 They replied,* **Believe in the Lord Jesus, and you will be saved**—*you and your household.*'"

Romans 10:9–11 say:

> "*9* **if you confess with your mouth, 'Jesus is Lord,' and believe in your heart that God raised him from the dead, you will be saved**. *10 For it is with your heart that you believe and are justified, and it is with your mouth that you confess and are saved. 11 As the Scripture says, 'Anyone who trusts in him will never be put to shame.'*"

First John 1:9 says:

*"⁹ If we confess our sins, he is faithful and just and will forgive us our sins and purify us from all unrighteousness."*

First, you must believe Jesus is the Son of God and that God raised him from the dead. Then you ask him to forgive you of your sins, ask him to come into your heart and life and be your Savior, and then confess that He is Lord of your life.

## Prayer for Salvation

If you have never asked Jesus into your heart to be the Lord of your life, you can pray this prayer:

*"Dear Lord Jesus, I know I am a sinner. Please forgive me of my sins and come into my heart and life. You said in Romans 10:9, 'If you confess with your mouth, 'Jesus is Lord,' and believe in your heart that God raised him from the dead, you will be saved." So I confess that You, Jesus, are my Lord and Savior, and I believe in my heart that You are the Son of God, You died on the cross for my sins, and God raised You from the dead. Now I give You my life. Please teach me Your ways and help me to serve You all of my life. Thank you for saving me and cleansing me of sin and making me your child. I give You praise, in Jesus' Name, Amen!"*

Now you are a new, born-again child of God! Praise the Lord! I encourage you to keep studying the Word of God every day to grow up spiritually and learn to live in the victory that God has prepared and provided for you every day of your life!

[2] See my book "The Story of God's Glorious Plan for Man"

[3] Peterson, Carl, M.D. "Medical Facts About Speaking In Tongues – Carl R. Peterson, M.D," *Being Part of the New Covenant*, June 14, 2011. Accessed October 27, 2022.

[4] Virkler, Mark. "Health Benefits of Speaking in Tongues." *Communion with God Ministries*, March 19, 2014. Accessed October 27, 2022.

[5] Carey, Benedict. "A Neuroscientific Look at Speaking in Tongues." *The New York Times*, November 7, 2006. Accessed March 4, 2016.

[6] Ibid.

# About the Author

By jumbo jet and small propeller plane, by ship, small boat, ferry and train, by truck, bus, jeepney, auto rickshaw, automobile, motorcycle, tricycle, and by foot, **Cherri Campbell** has been a traveling missionary in over twenty nations, teaching the Word of God and preaching in Bible schools, ministers' conferences, churches, youth conferences, and women's conferences. She is the author of a one-year Bible school curriculum called *Foundations of Victorious Living*, which has been adopted by several Bible schools. She has lived in the bush in Vanuatu, the Solomon Islands, Papua New Guinea, and the Federated States of Micronesia. She has preached and taught the Word of God in the underground church in Asia, traveled by train preaching across India, taught in conferences in the Himalayas, and preached in Bible schools, churches, and conferences in Southeast Asia, East Africa, and West Africa.

Cherri now lives in Colorado, and in 2013, she began a daily half-hour radio broadcast called *Victorious Faith*, which is also available on her website, *victoriousfaith.co*, and YouTube channel. Her simple yet in-depth teaching style has helped many Christians around the world, including pastors, gain a deeper understanding and practical application of the Word of God to receive healings, supernatural provision, victories, and breakthroughs in their own lives.

Cherri's calling is to train and equip the Body of Christ to live and operate *victoriously* in the Kingdom of God, maturing the saints to *be* a glorious and triumphant Church and to *do* the works of Jesus Christ.